The Weight of Snow

by

Sharon Lask Munson

BLUE LIGHT PRESS ❖ 1ST WORLD PUBLISHING

1ST WORLD
PUBLISHING

SAN FRANCISCO ❖ FAIRFIELD ❖ DELHI

The Weight of Snow

1st World Library
PO Box 2211
Fairfield, IA 52556
www.1stworldpublishing.com

Blue Light Press
www.bluelightpress.com
bluelightpress@aol.com

Book & Cover Design
Melanie Gendron
melaniegendron999@gmail.com

Cover Art
Bench in Snow, © Carol Dickie
www.caroldickiefineart.com

Author Photo
Keith Munson
munsonkeith@gmail.com

First Edition

Library of Congress Control Number: 2019933951

ISBN 9781421836232

In loving memory of my parents
Leon and Bernice Lask

To my husband Keith
my biggest fan

and to my sister Bonnie
who knows what's true
and what's fiction

Acknowledgments

Thanks to the editors of the following journals in which these poems appeared, sometimes in alternate versions.

The Absence of Something Specified: "Midwest Genesis"
Alimentum: "Kugel"
Califragile & Stillness Settles Down the Lane: "Two Chairs"
Cirque: " Heat"
Cirque: "Wade a Little Deeper, Darling"
Cirque: "Subject to Division"
Earth's Daughters: "Adjustment"
Earth's Daughters: "Along the Same Lines"
Earth's Daughters: "Self-Reproach"
Edge: "Happily Ever"
Evening Star Review: "Marriage 1955"
The Five-Two: "The New Woman"
Frogpond: "Star Sapphire"
Frogpond: "To a New Bride from Her Mother-in-Law"
Haibun Today: "Artifact"
Haibun Today: "Flight"
Haibun Today: "To a New Bride from Her Mother-in-Law"
Haibun Today: "Undercover"
Halfway Down the Stairs: "Moonstruck in Krogers"
It Demands a Wildness of Me: "Descendants"
It Demands a Wildness of Me: "Out on Her Own"
It Demands a Wildness of Me: "Redhead"
Light: "Hired Man"

Love Notes: "August Night at Crater Lake"

Love Poems: "Love, Decoded"

Penumbra: "Revealed

Penumbra & Braiding Lives: "She Woke to the Sound of Her
    Own Laughter"

Popshot: "Descendants

River Poet's Journal: "Possibilities"

Secrets and Dreams: "Dreaming, Someday I'd Marry the
    Lone Ranger"

Shooter: "A Woman Wouldn't Do It That Way"

Siblings; Our First Macrocosm: "Little Sister"

Spillway: "Filch"

Syracuse Cultural Workers Women Artists 2016 Datebook:
    "Checklist"

Syracuse Cultural Workers Women Artists 2019 Datebook:
    "Kindred Spirits"

Turn: "Winter Reflection"

The Way to My Heart: "Note on the Refrigerator"

World Enough Writers; Ice Cream: " Twinge"

Table of Contents

All Our Tomorrows

Prologue

Midwest Genesis

Midwesterners, choosing to move
to the Northwest, seldom go home.
They fly east for weddings, funerals,
show their children the old high school track field,
and where an early Dairy Queen sat on Main Street.

They brag about manageable seasons,
lack of heat and humidity, absence of snow.

They bike to work, become vegan,
drink herbal tea, take up running,
give up God for nature,
assume everyone is like-minded.

But in that uneasy sleep
just before waking,
they dream of golden wheat swaying in the wind,

sunflower fields as far as the eye can see,
hot summer sun on their necks,
hear their fathers ask,

How can you live
where they don't grow corn?

—Sharon Lask Munson

1

At the Juncture

Two Chairs

i

The watchmaker leans forward
in his metal desk chair,
lines up tools: drills,
files, brass hammers.
He slides one last dial
into a brown mailing envelope,
blinks back weariness.

Winter's frost painted windows
reflect a pale light.
He buttons his overcoat,
pulls on galoshes, gloves,
snaps off the overhead, bolts the door,

drives Woodward Avenue
crushed in bumper traffic
inching forward, heading home.

ii

The child kneels on a wooden chair,
coloring, as winter curls around the house.
Her landscape — emerald green grass,
sapphire sky, oversized flowers
in shades of amber, rose, sand.

She listens for his car on the drive,
crunch of tires, spitting ice;
sprints at the sound
of his key in the lock,
grate of the front door

and caught in mid-flight
her ribboned braids
sweep his cold, cold cheek.

Every September

mother buys my brown leather oxfords at Hudson's fourth floor children's shoe department. Year after year, Mr. Henderson waits on us. He measures my feet, remarks on their growth, never knowing I yearn for him to ask my choice regarding style, color.

        autumn harvest
        pencils the color of
        burnt-orange mums

Twinge

The dime I stole from her hairpin jar smoldered in my hand —
all the way to Mason's ice-cream parlor. The Dixie Cup vanilla
treat went down smoothly. I can still taste the wooden spoon.

Late Afternoon

The sun filters through gauzy curtains
creating shadows on the dining room floor.
Dust motes sway in the catch of light.

I am hurled airborne.
A giant tosses me up again and again.
He grasps me in mid air
as I snatch at his gold-braided
blue and white navy hat.
I feel the roughness of his uniform.

My aunts and uncles
seated around the kitchen table laugh.
Grandmother wipes a tear.
My baby sister, in her highchair, howls.
Our fox terrier runs circles
around the room, barking.

Mother leans against the wall,
hands in her apron pockets, smiling.
I never want the game to end.

I lift my arms to the giant.
He scoops me up.

Hired Man

Williams mowed our grass in summer,
pruned dead branches,
weeded, plucked spent flowers.
He cleaned gutters in autumn,
shoveled snow in winter.
In May he put screens on windows,
by October, took them down again.

During baseball season
I'd sit on the wooden steps,
keep him company while he worked,
both of us listening
to the portable Motorola on the porch,
cheering the Tigers at Briggs Stadium.

At noon he'd pull out his lunchbox.
I'd run into the house,
spread peanut butter on slices of Silvercup,
bring out two cold bottles of Rock and Rye.

Every December he walked up
the same porch steps, was invited in.
Dad would take down two shot glasses,
pour a bit of schnapps in each.

They toasted the holidays,
discussed recent snowstorms,
below zero predictions,
threatened strike at the Ford plant,
shook hands, wished each other a happy New Year.

Thinking back, I expect it was the times.
I never knew if *Williams*
was his first name or his last.

Ode to Parents Who Allow Such Magic

Old shingles have been pried away,
driveway swept, loose nails gathered.

Monday a new roof will be fastened in place,
but today is Sunday,

ideal for an expedition into the unknown.

Ladders lean against the house
sculpting shadows on siding.

Children climb toward the clouds
bearing paint, colored chalk,

trek beneath blue sky,
a safari to lands of sheer imagination.

Luke Skywalker and Princess Leia
spray-paint a fresco on bare plywood,

rainbows, flowers, hearts,

dispatch notes to spaceships,
message unknown planets,

conjure up new constellations,
create clusters of moons, scores of suns,

spend this perfect day
away from earthly concerns, spellbound.

Little Sister

It's my baby sister behind bars,
locked in for safety or convenience.
Probably both.

I'm three, standing outside the wooden playpen,
too old to be trapped
by the jail set up in the living room.

Through wooden spokes I slip in
my red rubber ball, a cloth alphabet book,
her favorite Raff the Giraffe rattle.

She inspects the offerings carefully
before passing them back,
thinks it's a game.

She holds a doll over her head and laughs.
A sultry summer wind wafts in through open windows.
White eyelet curtains flutter.

Late afternoon sun filters through,
fashions shadows.
The grandfather clock chimes four.

Dust motes hang in the light.
My baby sister grips the bars and tries to stand.
Letting go she laughs again.

I have no memory before her.

Each Passover

we recline at the dining room table while Father reads the story of the exodus: sweet wine is sipped, matzo eaten, bitter herbs nibbled, the youngest child asks the four questions, dinner is served

and somewhere between parsley dipped in salt water, and a brisket topped with prunes, Dad forgets, and year after year he hides the afikoman in the same silverware drawer. Given a nod, we children ignore the living room, den, and hallway in our race to the kitchen. The older cousins charge ahead. The swiftest wins the prize.

For everyone there's sponge cake sliced, fresh strawberries ladled, and always a new game next year.

> outside the window
> scent
> of hyacinth

Sabbath

The Cohen girls walk to synagogue each Saturday morning, appearing pious in somber long-sleeved, buttoned to the neck dresses. I know they are Orthodox — differing from our reformed Judaism — and assume God appreciates their faithful prayers on the same day he allows me to cruise the neighborhood on my red Schwinn.

I spend Saturdays riding down the steep incline of the Markowitz driveway, through the alley off Linwood, hunting silver foil from cigarette and chewing gum wrappers — working to make the largest silver ball in the neighborhood — believe God is quite pleased with me, too.

Undercover

When her mother leaves the house, the child walks into the large hall closet, pulls down the stairway leading to the attic, and climbs up into the cold musty space at the top of the house.

A mahogany buffet sits to the right of the entrance, its drawers filled with photos of strangers, faded letters tied in black ribbon, a scattering of hairpins, and a leather change purse filled with foreign coins. In a secret space behind the photos rests a filigree brooch, a gentleman's pocket watch, one extra long string of pearls, and a tattered Star of David — yellow threads still attached. Best, is a trunk packed with evening dresses she carefully slips on and gazes at herself in a cracked mirror stored along the wall.

Her ear is attuned to the front door. When she hears the creak and grate she scampers down. On the few occasions her mother asks if she had been in the attic, the child blinks her blue eyes in astonishment.

Periphery

at twelve

Woodhull Lake at dawn —
gunmetal gray, smooth and still.
Wooden cottages dot the shoreline.
Red Egrets gather on the raft.
Rowboats mark time.

By ten, the public beach
swarms with sunbathers.
I spend my mornings floating
in shallow waters, hunting shells,
constructing castles in sand.

Afternoons, I gape at teens
rubbing Coppertone on crisp bodies,
watch them play hide and seek
under cotton beach towels.

At night, pulled in by the music,
I head to the Big House,
the lake's historic dance hall;

stand outside in the shadows
where ghosts of Tommy Dorsey and Glen Miller
swing and sway with Sammy Kaye.

Couples rock and roll to *Great Balls of Fire*,
dance low and slow to *Blueberry Hill*.
Hoods in jeans loiter in the doorway,
practice scowling, smoke Camels, sip beer.

I dither at the juncture, unsure,
still safely on the far side, peeking in.

Dreaming, Someday I'd Marry the Lone Ranger

I spent my childhood with a toy six-shooter on each hip, repeater caps deep in my pockets, official junior deputy certificate on the bedroom wall, a tin star pinned to my Brownie uniform.

The day I meet my own buckaroo, he wears tan khakis, a white shirt, sleeves rolled to the elbows. Hankering to stroke the golden hairs on his arm, I look down to discover his size ten feet — clad in hand-made, black cherry, Lucchese, cowboy boots.

> twin buttes
> beyond Green River
> strong westerly winds

Gift of Hours

Twice a day for two years
my father drove to Wayne State,

delivering me on campus
in time for an early morning class,

collecting me after five
in front of the student union.

Together in the gray Dodge,
an hour in traffic each way,

we would discuss the day's events,
his words flowing softly:

strike at Ford's River Rouge,
Governor Romney's state income tax,

my term paper on *Sister Carrie*,
his worries as business slacked.

Sometimes he'd tell tales
from childhood,

Berlin, first time in an elevator:
glass doors, the city below,

the kind Antwerp tutor,
teaching Flemish,

Baron Rothchild's tea
for immigrant children in London.

We shared stories
over the hum of tires, rumble of exhausts,

bumper to bumper
on the John Lodge Freeway.

I understood even then
his words meant everything,

the blessing of his voice.

Possibilities

If she had accepted the teddy bear
on her sixteenth birthday,
his pin on her seventeenth,
a diamond at eighteen,
she would have walked down the aisle
a mere nineteen—a modest, very good girl.

She'd be living still
in a white Georgian house
within a gated community, overlooking
half an acre of nicely mowed grass.

She would plant tidy gardens
of heirloom roses in the back yard,
pretty pansies in pots by the front,

have a Picasso print from his blue period
bought to match her one of a kind couch.

She would have attended
her fiftieth high school reunion,
seated at the banquet table
with the very same girls
she had lunched with every Wednesday
for the last five decades,

dreamily picking at crumbs
while eyeing tea leaves
on the bottom of her cup,
reading into the brown remnants
all that could have been.

ii

She never married at nineteen,
never married at all.
Instead, took a midnight flight to Istanbul,
rented a sunny room
by the shore of the Bosphorus,
got used to the sound of foghorns
interrupting her sleep.

She found she loved the cries of the seagulls,
spicy smells of the city,
modern museums set within
mazes of pencil-shaped domes.

She opened a Turkish bakery
by the markets of the Grand Bazaar
where she specialized in spinach pastries,
puddings with saffron,
strong coffee, crowned with froth
served in tiny cups.

She lived out her long life
in the arms of turbaned men
who whispered words
in languages she didn't quite grasp

died sixty years later
in a bed strewn with poppies,
crocuses, cyclamen, and cosmos.

2

Slender Strands

Moonstruck in Krogers

She pushes her grocery cart toward Produce, slows to slip six cin-
namon-brown Bosc pears into a bag, but moves quickly enough
to keep him in view — his wide shoulders, tight jeans, shock of
rusty hair. She smiles all the way to the checkout.

> end of day
> strewn
> with possibilities

Winter Reflection

We select a table for two by the window, a stone's toss from the restaurant's crackling fire. The clear glass sends back a dual image. The blaze within intermingles with December's white winter camellias blooming beyond the pane, dense bouquets of glassy leaves, fragile petals.

Bowed by relentless rain this cold wet evening, the flame, like a cunning serpent, sheds its skin and consumes.

Heat

Gallatin River, Montana

Not a single stonefly rises.
Even the trout swim out of sight
moving deep into pools
behind mossy boulders
and sunken Ponderosa pines.

The river tumbles downstream.
We listen to the music of small rapids,
strain of a Western Meadowlark,
hum of insects beyond the huckleberry.

On the far side of the whitewater
we discover a grassy cove
cloaked by tall cottonwoods,
fall sleep in the afternoon.

Later you fan me
with the brim of your Stetson
as I lie in the shadow
of the Rockies, watch
two dark-winged butterflies
on a Star Lily leaf.

Waylay

I ambush him with a shot of Jameson's. Add single malt whiskey
to freshly brewed Café del Mundo, stir in a trace of sugar, hint
of vanilla. Whip fresh cream to stiff peaks before crowning tall
glass mugs.

His hand, rugged and cold as glacial ice, warms. Through the
picture window we contemplate the snow-capped mountains of
the Chugach Range.

> white on white
> blue sweep
> of winter sky

Happily Ever

i

The average wedding in America today
costs often half a year's salary,
nearly $35,329 dollars.

Checklist

banquet hall
bar service
        domestic   imported
bride's bouquet
bride's dress
bridesmaid's presents
caterer
confetti
engraved thank you cards
event fee
florist
groom men's presents
guest favors
hair and make-up
hors d'oeuvres
initialed napkins
invitations
leather bound album
live band
justice of the peace, minister, rabbi
photographer
rehearsal dinner
rings
save-the-date-cards
sit down dinner

wedding cake
wedding planner

destination honeymoon
that are so popular —
white sand beaches
                    Hawaii
                    Mexico
                    the Caribbean

          ii

I wore a pink wool, short-sleeved dress
on sale in the *Better Wear* department
of Northern Commercial,
went to City Hall on a Friday,
brought four friends to witness,
celebrated at the Captain Cook
toasting the day with sparkling wine

and the *cake*
homemade raspberry pie.
made from wild Alaskan berries, hand picked.

Called my parents.

Our honeymoon — a Saturday morning drive
up the Glenn Highway
to Gunsight Mountain for stacks of
sourdough pancakes, maple syrup, coffee.

To a New Bride from Her Mother-in-Law

My dear, I must advise, we invite friends *to* dinner, not *for* dinner. At formal parties, use white linen. Colorful cotton is too casual. Placemats are best left for breakfast or lunch. When setting the table, choose a low centerpiece. One suggestion would be heads of white hydrangeas spilling from a shallow bowl. Of course, these considerations are seasonal.

When shopping for beef, ring for the butcher. He will cut your roast to order. As to side dishes, be aware of freshness and color. Never serve tinned; frozen, only in an emergency. Include a green vegetable with every evening meal. A second offering might be a corn soufflé, orange yams stuffed with mixed fruit, or a dish of garden beets. You'll be surprised at how many people think they dislike beets, but in a fragrant and colorful sauce, the crimson colored root will have most guests coming back for more.

After dinner, lead your guests into the front room. End the meal with hot tea around the fireplace. Serve lemon slices with a light Darjeeling or smooth Earl Grey. You may also offer the choice of cream with a hearty Assam if serving fish or dairy. Buy a sturdy brass tea trolley with a glass top. Fine china sparkles on glass.

> one perfect pear
> on crystal
> autumn's reflection

Star Sapphire

As they pull up the old Berber, she kneels, searches the wooden floor for a stone that fell out of a filigree ring a decade ago. She spots sewing pins, two pearl buttons, a bent buffalo nickel, but nothing that reminds her of her lover's eyes at midnight.

        branches
        almost bare
        trill of a warbler

Drawing Open Blinds

Early morning. The sun begins its rounds, painting the room a warm shade of maroon. The metal chain of the neighbor's beagle scrapes across their cement patio. Floorboard heaters begin to rumble. Sliding into slippers, I tread downstairs.

The newspaper waits by the front door, rubber banded. I microwave a serving of oatmeal, sprinkle nuts, cranberries. Before eating, I make a sweep through the house; draw open blinds. Two cyclists make a sharp turn around the cul-de-sac. Quarrel of sparrows peck at my feeder.

The grass looks a darker green, the pavement slightly wet. I move to the table, gather pink tulip petals from the tablecloth, blow away scatterings of pollen.

Presence

This world is but a canvas to our imagination.
— Henry David Thoreau

i

The boy scales a narrow ledge of the cliff. Reaching for a sharp stone, he carves an antelope into the yellow sandstone, chisels three deer running through the brush. He outlines hunters on a chase, a short-tailed quail and thick-bodied rattlesnakes. Higher up the steep rock-face he scratches a crescent moon, three stars.

ii

SHRIEK is the tag spray-painted black on the new city hall. Geometrical shapes in dazzling colors — chartreuse, cobalt, and blood red surround the letters. The young man works by the beam of the streetlight — quickly, hand steady, eyes fixed. Finished, he eyeballs his artistry, gathers up the paint cans, and darts into the night.

Self-Reproach

Because he is going to shower, I remove the small lump of soap left in the dish, replace it with a fresh sweet smelling bar of Camay. Guilt like a cloudburst intercedes, the waste.

Raised the child of working parents, I preserve all slender strands until they become thin and transparent, slipping invisibly down the drain.

Perspective

Come here he cries from the living room. *Hurry.* She hears the urgency, abandons her hot tea and hastens down the hall. *Hurry!* She imagines a heart attack, stroke, broken arm.

The television's set to his favorite auto auction. *Look*, he declares with longing as a silvery-blue convertible advances along a red carpet. *A 1939 Hudson*, he exclaims. *Only three ever existed and this is the last survivor.*

She lingers, drawn to the boy in him.

Love, Decoded

i

It's chilly today,
snow blankets the roof,
the sky gunmetal gray,
real winter weather

code for slow simmering soup for dinner;
rich beef broth studded
with a rainbow of Walla-Walla onions,
diced tomatoes, thinly sliced zucchini,
scattering of pasta,
splash of red wine.

Code for, *I love you.*
I'll take care of you in my way.

ii

My lover leaves a package
on the kitchen counter, a surprise
wrapped in plum-colored tissue.

Upon opening, I find
a dark indigo shirt,
the cozy flannel embellished
with an embroidered teacup
surrounded by carefully stitched sprays
of sweet peas, violets, ivy.

Steam from the cup
soars over the soft pima cotton
in the shape of a large red heart.

Code, again.

Note on the Refrigerator

after William Carlos Williams

I've made rice pudding for your birthday, your favorite — sweet, smooth, studded with dark raisins, slow-baked to a golden custard. Indulge me, always the missing spoonful.

Wade a Little Deeper, Darling

i

Decades later he will tell her
how difficult it was,
the two of them fly fishing together

her lines getting caught in tree branches,
snagging rocks on the bottom of rivers.

His time spent untangling,
removing fish from hooks,
retying flies to leaders.

But he was young,
in the beginnings of their marriage,
hesitant to speak.

ii

What she had really wanted
was a smooth flat spot on a wide log,
stretches of time to listen to water
eddy around a bank,
hear the music of songbirds,

observe the sun glaring off the water
like a million stars ricocheting,
study a hatch of mayflies rising
as rainbow trout snatch them in mid air,

to marvel as she watched
her young husband cast a line,
the bend of his bamboo rod,
a horseshoe for luck

time to sit against a slate-gray pine,
letting the lazy day take shape.

Marriage 1952

Early dawn, on the day of her wedding
she slides into jeans, sneakers,
mounts her red Schwinn,
rides LaSalle Boulevard

resolving, with each turn of the wheel
to toss away parental approval,
curfews, permission,
entrusting all her tomorrows to her husband

unaware she'll hand over weekly paychecks,
shopping receipts,
serve dinner precisely at six

until early one misty morning
as she twirls her thick blond hair
into his favorite pageboy

she takes a step forward,
peers closely at an errant curl
that seems to have run away

fades in the fog
of her full-length bathroom mirror
and disappears.

Revealed

I thought he must be her third or fourth. One never asks. A whirlwind romance she had told me. When I met her new husband I was dumbstruck, gazed upon a Cary Grant look alike: tall, thin, an imposing man. His dark hair lay neatly parted. His blue-striped shirt starched, collar button-down. He took my hand with an old-fashioned demeanor. His roguish smile was like riots of color in an untamed garden.

> warm breeze
> in the sultry air
> scent of sweet peas

I see her alone in theaters, restaurants, about town. Her wide brimmed hat eclipses a solitary figure. She tells me he has his own ways. A lifetime of habits! Stays in at night. Goes to bed early. Doesn't try new foods. Won't sample curry, cumin, or cardamom. Doesn't care for garden fresh or green. Every night he makes his own dinner: ham and cheese on white bread, dab of yellow mustard, chips, canned soup. He eats in front of the television, watching football every autumn. During other seasons he varies the sports: basketball, baseball, golf. She eats alone at the kitchen table, turning pages.

> breath catching cold
> hoarfrost
> on fence posts

Adjustment

He opens all letters addressed to her
he was once in charge at work

itemizes their checkbook
cleans out hall closets

thins her collection
of out-of-print books.

She hides her lined journal
in the kitchen near the back door

on the bottom shelf
behind the green bowl

talks on her cell phone
in the dim of the garage.

But things are getting better, she says.
We're working on it.

She roams neighborhood malls on long afternoons
filling her days alone

while he signs up for classes for both of them
subjects he's eager to take for himself

joins organized tours
with busloads of strangers

alphabetically lines up
cupboards of canned goods

rearranges porch furniture
pulls up old roses.

But things are getting better she says.
We're working on it.

Plumage

When company visits, he has a dozen long-stemmed red roses delivered from the most expensive florist in town.

As a newlywed she'd gather them close, inhale their bouquet, bring out her Waterford, select the most conspicuous spot in the room to show off his ardor.

Years later, she calls to their housekeeper — *answer the door, do something with them.*

> iridescence
> a peacock's fan
> dulls

Subject to Division

Before another night of arguments, threats, ultimatums,
she stuffs an overnight bag, tiptoes downstairs,
steals out as the clock chimes midnight.

After the separation he claims ownership
of the twelve place settings of blue Wedgewood
he had once thought her extravagant to buy,

antique miniatures she had spent a decade collecting,
her grandmother's hand crocheted ecru bedspread
unfurled in the guest room, upstairs.

After the divorce he feels he had the upper hand,
potentate of possessions,
trappings of bits and pieces.

He moves through silent rooms fondling, caressing.
She asks for nothing — soars away,
light and unencumbered.

The Weight of Snow

On the day of his funeral she slips into sweats, embarks on her early morning training: sit ups, bench presses, leg curls — before driving six miles to keep her weekly wash and set. When the beautician asks what's new, she replies, *my husband died Thursday.*

Under the dryer she riffles through pages of *Ladies Day*, closes her eyes, lets the warmth lull her into sleep. Later she wanders into Bloomingdales, tries on high-necked woolly sweaters for the bitter January afternoon ahead.

Luckily, her hair falls into enough disarray to make her look properly mournful at the funeral.

3

All Our Tomorrows

A Woman Wouldn't Do It That Way

A man would use a forty-five,
splatter blood on walls, carpets,
leave smears and splotches
for someone else to clean up.

A woman would seldom leave disorder.
She might shower first,
slip on a fresh nightgown,
swallow pills with something sweet
to mask the taste,
brush her teeth,
slide between fresh-smelling sheets
letting the lightness of down
shepherd her into oblivion.

Or she might bundle up
on a cold snowy night,
head to the river, to a spot
where the ice is thin and brittle
and dark waters entice — tread carefully
until she launches herself

softening the heartache
for those left behind
to speak softly of

such a tragic accident.

Flight

Wonderful, I hear him say to the waitress as he holds the wine up to bright daylight, swirls the Cabernet, lifts the stem to his nose, closes one nostril and sniffs, closes the other, sniffs again. Chocolate, he calls out. *No, cherry with a hint of vanilla* he proclaims before taking a sip. He sucks in as if pulling through a straw, circulating the red wine throughout his mouth, pretending with the first tasting he knows more than he actually does. He holds the waitress captive as she rolls her eyes and listens impatiently to him pontificating upon wines he has sampled in Spain, France, Romania, announcing he sometimes sends a bottle back to prove his point.

> hummingbird
> iridescent lime and jade
> at my feeder

Out of the Blue

     i

I swerve to the right,
avoid hitting the blue bunny
in the middle of the road.

The bunny, blue and furry,
in all likelihood
purchased for a boy.

Some parents code in pink and blue
although the custom is waning.

     ii

My friend Penny opted for beige, a neutral color
determined not to influence her child

wanting him to grow up
in a less sexist world,
desiring to quash stereotypes.

Her son, brought up with both
dolls and trucks, footballs and jump ropes,
his nursery, a dazzling rainbow,

at eighteen months stood on the bench seat
of his father's new red Toyota pick-up truck,

grabs the steering wheel,
digs in his heels,
arches his back,

and utters sounds
never before heard out of his soft rosy mouth

VAARRROOOMMMMM
            VAARRROOOMMMMMM
                    VAARRROOOMMMMM

Of Weather

i

An easy winter my neighbor remarks
raking last fall's leaves from yellow crocuses.
January's sunshine, February's clear skies,
folks out-of-doors in March,
coats unbuttoned, flapping in mild breezes
like sandpipers skimming blue waters.

ii

Snow in the valley comes as a surprise.
Almost April, and the sea of white,
weighty as weariness, blankets
woodland, back country, city streets,
all bowed down in astonishment.

Fragile pink blossoms perish, iced over.
Jagged bare limbs, splintered and raw
poke out, ghost-like,
silhouettes against the ashen sky.

Filch

She waters the lone geranium on the window ledge, washes paint jars and brushes, tidies shelves, wipes the blackboard, cleans erasers, places corrected math into a wire basket, slips papers to check into her bag.

She slides into boots, slips on her coat, hat, scarf. She reaches for the large Red Delicious apple-for-the-teacher someone gave her that morning, the snack she planned to eat in the car on the way home. She sees one fair-sized tooth-marked bite on the backside.

> flurry of snowflakes
> through evening shadows
> peel of laughter

Early Morning Draft

Alert to the faint chime
of the clock downstairs
she counts to three,

broods over the belated birthday card
never mailed
still sitting on the kitchen counter,

frets over the red warning light
on the Buick's dash.
By four a.m. she's resigned,

concentrates on the muted hum
from Delta Highway's thrum of tires,
rumble of engines, roar of tailpipes,

imagines a night worker
driving home to his lover's bed
or a young soldier airport bound
for an early morning flight.

She hears the wail of a siren, imagines
flames illuminating the dark, possibly an
ambulance transporting a sick child.

She rotates her pillow,
roots around for a cool spot,
concede defeat,

pushes the blanket aside,
rummages under the bed for slippers,
shuffles across the hall,

wakes her sleeping computer
and plunges into this new poem.

Elegy

She was an accomplished cook
declare well-used copper cookware
suspended over the kitchen island,

a woman of small stature
remark size-five wedges
neglected on the steps,

keen reader
carefully selected novels
lining cluttered shelves respond,

valued beauty
blue Lenox dishes
stored in the maple hutch boast,

respectful of nature
note bird feeders
dangling from the red maple,

loved sunshine,
comments the living room's
broad picture window,

devoted mother,
the child's playhouse
in the backyard bellows,

friendly neighbor
chatter twisting pathways from the garden
to a home next door.

But the old house
attentive to the silence whispers,
but the singing's gone.

Breakfast

Breakfast alone at a neighborhood café.
Breakfast quiet — bring a book.
Breakfast light, fruit and yogurt.
Breakfast heavy, pancakes and bacon.

Have a meal at a truck stop.
On another day try the Ritz.
Breakfast at a window table
as January snow blankets the city.

Sip a café crème, nibble a jelly doughnut
with the Sunday comics.
Breakfast on a patio or in the garden.
Plan birthday brunches; invite a crowd.

Order savory crepes at the Space Needle.

In Paris, plan a breakfast picnic
on the Champs de Mars.
Bring a buttery croissant, a mimosa in a thermos.
Toast the Eiffel Tower. Toast the day.

Take the Chunnel to London.
Overnight at Claridge's!
Order an in-room breakfast,
smoked salmon scramble and potato cakes.

Breakfast while the fish are rising
and the sun's just coming up.
Grill fresh rainbow trout
over the campfire.

Breakfast as the stock market rises — or falls.

Pack a breakfast of sandwiches.
Share with the person pushing a cart on Broadway.
Request coddled eggs with your great aunt,
waffles with a child.

Breakfast with your favorite poet.
If you oversleep, have breakfast for lunch.

Redhead

When they talk of their high school days, I hear them speak of Rochelle, the classmate they all fancied — her hair, a shade that wasn't carroty, but more auburn or russet. Her long tresses cascaded in great waves, like the ocean sweeping to shore on the heels of a winter storm, drifting over the smooth pale of her cheeks as wispy strands catch the sunlight entering study hall windows.

We meet at a 50th high school reunion; her thinning silver hair is cropped short. She tells me, with retirement upon her, she has a hunger to learn Italian. We speak of rereading favorite classics. We call out Jane Austen in unison.

She asks, during a lull in our conversation, if my dark brown hair is custom blended in a salon.

Veneer

They dress her in beige: stretch pants, a sweatshirt, another resident's name sewn into the collar. She is wheeled into breakfast garbed in a shade that would have horrified her, one that makes her skin sallow. A hue that is not on her color-chart! I think back to her brightly lit walk-in closet, dresses hanging next to slacks and shirts, shoes lined up by height, scarves and bags color coded, the entire space more vivid than a double rainbow in a deep blue sky — hot magenta, crimson, violet, aquamarine, Persian rose.

> dusk
> streaks of fuchsia
> pierce pink clouds

Henry and Me

i

Growing up in the same small town,
we left to explore the world.
I headed north, he south,
kept in touch via postcards,
occasional phone calls.

At his sudden death I fly home,
feel like an interloper at his funeral,
a service organized by strangers.

A small number of his relatives show up:
a few elderly cousins, a great-nephew,
an aged aunt with her mind unavailable.
Not even the minister knew him well.

His obit ran in the *Daily Gazette*.
Old neighbors gather on these occasions,
sing "Amazing Grace" with gusto,
enjoy a free potluck meal.

ii

With my nomadic life behind me,
even fewer will line up when I die.
All I have are casual workmates
and my Saturday morning breakfast group.

Think I'll skip my own funeral,
find someone to scatter
my ashes into wind and water

preferably near The Thumb in Michigan,
into the cold depths of Lake Huron.
I'll track down a scrap of my heart
unleashed accidentally years earlier.

I've always relished relocating.

Harold and Agnes

Late in years, my great-uncle suggested to a longtime employee she care for him until the end. If willing, she would inherit everything. Agnes agreed. For twelve years she rustled up hot oatmeal each morning, chicken on Friday, waxed and buffed his kitchen floor, filled in at the poker table, played hostess to nieces and nephews. She held his hand and wept at his last breath at ninety-six.

She never moved from the house, spent little. She donated to the poor, endowed the community college, subsidized after school programs. In death, what was left, she returned to his family.

> falling snow
> gentle
> as a kiss

Kugel

They sit in the resident's lounge
discussing the trip earlier that day
to a senior luncheon.

They had been served chopped liver, roast brisket,
kugel, and an apple-raisin strudel for dessert.
The entertainment; a discussion
on the life and writings of Philip Roth.

But it is the beloved kugel
claiming the late afternoon's conversation.
No two kugels are cut from the same dough.

In the days Leah kept house
her kugel was made with broad noodles,
eggs, golden raisins, brown sugar, farmer's cheese,
walnuts, and a hint of cinnamon.

Esther preferred medium noodles —
cream cheese, dark raisins,
two generous cups of chopped green apples.

Dinah relied on her own mother's recipe
brought, *before the war*, from Poland;
noodles any size. But what set the dish apart;
dry cottage cheese, black prunes,
and the cookie crumb topping her children loved.

Mona modernized, cut calories,
yogurt instead of sour cream,
halved the number of eggs,
added dried apricots and whatever other fruit
she had stored in the pantry.

Sophie shied away from sweet puddings.
Her husband, *May his memory be for a blessing*,
favored savory sides. She made vegetable kugels,
spinach or potatoes as the main ingredient.

As the winter day darkened, Rose divulged
she was partial to small-curd cottage cheese,
adding two hard cheeses: Swiss
and a liberal shower of parmesan.

At five o'clock sharp
the dinner bell was heard
and the ladies quickly marched into the dining room
with very good appetites, indeed.

Out on Her Own

She stops me at the crosswalk
of Main & Chequessett Neck Road,
grips my hand, a regular Charles Atlas hold.

The stooped, bird-like
white-haired crone in rumpled pink
has a story to tell.
Her stance commands onlookers
to gather, cars to slow.

She relays the same account
she must have told a hundred times
to other unsuspecting souls, caught
in the lattice of her jumbled web.

The specifics of her narrative
not interesting enough
to repeat in this small poem

but the twinge I feel
when I recognize the dire straits
of this befuddled old stranger makes me linger,

her gnarled hand in mine
until the end of her tale.

Harmonica

At dusk, the river rushes
through Alton Baker Park,
sweeps away fallen branches,
broken limbs, pays no heed
to the bluster of March winds.

Beside the channel,
two men settle on a cedar bench.
Stooped, heads down,
absorbed in the moment,
they stroke metal reeds along the length
of their small mouth organs.

Traffic from the highway filters through,
joins the easygoing strains of Moon River;
two drifters off to see the world,
the ageless two-part harmony welcomes night.

Kindred Spirit

Hello, mumbles a hesitant
grizzled voice. *Hello, Mama.*
I tell the caller he has the wrong number.
Two weeks later he calls again.

The third call comes on a slow afternoon.
This time I feel we are somehow linked.
I introduce myself and tell him he's called before.
He apologizes.

We begin slowly—speak of small things:
warm weather, peaches in summer, lack of rain.

I ask about his life.
Grew up on a small farm, he volunteers.
Not much in schooling, but we worked hard.
Mama worked in the fields.
I helped Pa with the sheep.

He calls sporadically for over a year.
I never put him off.
I never claim to be his mama.
We speak of work, seasons of the year.
He discusses planting and harvesting.
I reflect on the primroses
planted in pots by my front door.

The last called is brief.
Moments after my telephone rings
a woman's voice barks at me,
says the calls won't be continuing,
tells me she's the caregiver and he's confused.

I'm uneasy about my cellular companion.
Days later, I punch in the number
saved in my phone's memory.
It had been disconnected.

She Woke to the Sound of Her Own Laughter

and in that moment, *if* she had woken him to speak of her dream, she could have carried the vision all day: the train to Istanbul, the dining car, polished wood, starched linen, heft of crystal, the sleek Gatsby dress on her back — chocolate silk, onyx beading.

If she carried the dream all day, she could have tried on different beginnings, endings: the Turkish Sultan, the charade, murder, double-deal trickery, perhaps an escape through the old walled city — uncertainty that made the danger so thrilling. She could have lived a fable or an epic poem.

But as she lay there, with laughter on her lips, she nodded off, and on wakening, the dream was gone, her mouth, dry.

angle of moonlight, parted curtains

Artifact

She saves her mother's hair in a shoebox stored in the cellar; long auburn tresses frosted with silver, tightly braided.

In a dream she loosens the interlaced strands, breathes in the scent of White Diamonds, runs her fingers through what was glossy and sleek.

She wakes to the memory of her own long brown hair jerked into pigtailed compliance: the tug, the yank, the jab of a barrette.

> brittle leaves
> underfoot
> dust rising

Along the Same Lines

Step on a crack,
break your mother's back.
Old Children's Game

We took the superstition seriously,
walked with friends down Burlingame Street,
skipped over lines.

At school, we lined up for lunch,
water fountain, pencil sharpener.
We scurried to be head of the line.

Gym lines were a challenge —
relays to run, bars to jump, ropes to climb,
lines of scrimmage, finishing lines.

We wrote on lined paper,
discussed story lines,
studied plus & minus signs.

We sat in desks all aligned,
stayed within margins as we underlined,
outlined, colored within or outside the lines.

Bad grades
meant borderline.
Teachers took a tough line.

Times change.
We no longer use clotheslines,
talk on party lines or wear hosiery, the seamed kind.

Now we have wrinkle lines,
laugh lines, crow's feet,
mouths set in angry lines.

We line up for movies,
park cars within parallel lines,
jog the path, run the track,

line our pockets,
question a person's line of work,
their bloodlines.

We fight wars on front lines,
hold defense lines,
remember the Maginot Line.

When drowning, we grab lifelines,
consider span of lives,
scribble verse in lines.

We blur lines
between news and entertainment,
depend on cable lines.

Organizations expect us
to follow rules, behave accordingly,
fall into line.

The Internet
gives us invisible
world wide wireless lines.

We live our lives
& when times gets hard
we lay it all out — on the line.

Autumn Colors

We haven't changed a bit I say to my husband of forty years as I dust the walnut frame that holds our wedding photo. He stares at me blankly. His amazement turns into a slow smile that turns into a wide grin as he opens his arms and I slide right in. I was right in my way. Little has changed.

Timekeeper

I have a collection of vintage wristwatches,
meshed gears and springs,
emblems of art and science.

Few masters remain to repair these timepieces,
fingers to probe the movement, peer through a loupe.
Only a handful of experts left with a light touch.

I wore my oval Wittnauer during high school,
the Gruen marcasite, a graduation gift.
My treasured rhinestone studded Elgin
with its slim black leather band
was on my wrist the night Ringo shook my hand.

I have my father's gold plated
Longines pocket watch
given to him by *his* father

and the well worn railroad watch
belonging to my husband's great-great uncle,
still meeting precise accuracy standards.

Even battery-operated, throw away
timepieces have become obsolete
since the spread of the cell phone —
these wireless devices connecting the world

without changing the fact
that time continues to move forward
like a river, never back.

The New Woman

She telephones, speaks
of her husband's best friend
arriving at their door with his new woman
three months after his wife's death.

The revelation explodes through the air
as she whispers details
while seven hundred miles away
I lower my voice in accordance

collaborating on what is acceptable
after a forty-year marriage,
mumbling about decency.

Of course it's ourselves we're thinking of,
tossing out numbers,
the length of time a man should wait
when a homemade casserole is hand delivered
or pink straps slip from pale plump shoulders.

We dither between six or nine months,
agreeing that a least at year should pass
before he thinks of a successor

plotting that very night
to have serious discussions at our own kitchen tables,
probably ruining two very good dinners

and if the conversations
don't lead to satisfactory conclusions

we'll confer again,
discuss large caliber handguns,
razor-edged hunting knives,
a bit of arsenic in steel-cut oats.

Checklist

Mostly, she talks. I listen.
Her voice, the music of my childhood —
the pitch, the cadence, all Aunt Hattie.

We talk of Mollie's temper,
Uncle Harold's triumphs,
Norman's business failures,
and whatever happened to
cousin Mildred's daughter,
the middle one who went to Stanford
and showed such promise.

She tells me to buy canned tuna
in olive oil at Trader Joe's.
She tells me to stop spreading with schmaltz,
it will kill me.
She tells me on Christmas Day
all the Jews in town
will be dining in Chinese restaurants.
At ninety, she's a regular Fanny Brice.

After I'm dead, she tells me,
Sheldon will pass the bar.
Ruthie will meet someone and remarry.
Call and let me know.

Visit

Red maple leaves fall on your graves.
Reaching into my pocket, I leave two small
stones from my garden to let you know I've
been here.

> final note
> all the questions
> I never asked

Descendants

i

Our children, of course,
retain memories, loving or not.

Grandchildren might remember
the pipe smell of Dunhill-London

or sugar cookie dough
rolled out on a kitchen counter.

For great-grandchildren
a framed portrait

tucked away in the linen closet
is merely that of a stranger

something to be added
to garage sale odds and ends

along with the chipped Wedgewood
no one in the family wants.

ii

A great-great grandchild
rummaging in a local junk shop

might spy a familiar likeness, framed,
heart shaped face, jutting chin,

widow's peak,
something about the mouth, the jaw

and on a whim
claim the old canvas

hang it beside a corner bookcase
filled with used novels bought in bulk

to make a new home ageless.

About the Author

Sharon Lask Munson was born and raised in Detroit, Michigan. She taught school in England, Germany, Okinawa, and Puerto Rico before driving to Anchorage, Alaska and staying for the next twenty years. She is a retired teacher, poet, coffee addict, old movie enthusiast, lover of road trips — with many published poems, two chapbooks, and one full-length book of poetry. She now lives and writes in Eugene, Oregon.

She says many things motivate her to write: a mood, a memory, the smell of cooking, burning leaves, a windy day, rain, fog, something observed or overheard — and of course, imagination. She has a pin that says, "I Make Things Up."

You can find her at www.sharonlaskmunson.com

.

www.ingramcontent.com/pod-product-compliance
Lightning Source LLC
Chambersburg PA
CBHW032025090426
42741CB00006B/736